D0271853

Simple Weaving

Also by Marthann Alexander

WEAVING ON CARDBOARD

Simple Weaving

MARTHANN ALEXANDER

TAPLINGER PUBLISHING COMPANY
NEW YORK

Second Printing

Published in the United States by
TAPLINGER PUBLISHING CO., INC.
New York, New York

Library of Congress Catalog Card Number: 68-17470

ISBN 0-8008-7200-2

Foreword

There is a need today for creative handwork. The use of threads and yarns presents an opportunity for the individual to express himself creatively in design and color. It is a thrill to build a loom and weave a piece of fabric, watching the threads develop into an original creation.

The weaving devices included here are presented to give the inexperienced a taste of simple weaving. The methods are not all weaving techniques in the strictest sense of the word, but they produce cords, bands, and fabrics of very simple construction. Emphasis is placed on the simplicity of the weaving device. Very few special tools are needed to construct all the looms presented here.

These methods have been successfully used in presenting weaving to children in Indiana public schools and to adults. Children in the intermediate grades take an immediate interest in weaving and succeed quickly. Best results are obtained by reading through the entire chapter before the loom is constructed or weaving is attempted. Then carefully follow the directions given for building the loom and weaving.

The material is based on notes gathered and used by the author over a period of years, both as a student of weaving in this country and as a traveler studying weaving in Guatemala and Mexico. Some of the material was used in an original research paper for a Master's Degree in Art Education at Ball State Teachers College.

The author extends her thanks to Lily Mills for the use of threads for photographs, Dr. Fred Schmidt for his encouragement, Merl George who took the photographs, and to the ten-year old children who posed for most of the photographs and were so thrilled to learn to weave.

Marthann Alexander

Contents

1	Hungarian Weaving	9
2	Weaving on a Hosiery Box	17
3	Finger Weaving	25
4	Spool Weaving	31
5	The Slot Loom	39
6	The T-D Loom	45
7	Waffle Weaving	53
8	Weaving on the Flat Loom	57
9	Card Weaving	63
10	Weaving on a Fruit Lug	71
11	Weaving with Loopers	75
12	The Twine Rug	79
13	A Shag Rug on an Orange Crate	85
14	Ojibway Indian Bag Loom	89
15	Inkle Weaving	93
16	Cardboard Weaving	99
17	Threading the Two-Harness Loom	105
	Glossary of Weaving Terms	109
	Suggestions for Color Harmony	111

Simple Weaving

CHAPTER I

Let's Try Some Hungarian Weaving

Hungarian weaving is a type of braiding which is ideally suited to children nine, ten, or eleven years old. It may be done in a finer form by junior high school age children. The cloth may be produced in a narrow width or in a wide band, according to the weight of thread used and the closeness of the tacks or brads on the one-piece loom, Fig. 1.

The loom is a simple arrangement of finishing nails standing upright on a base of plywood. A narrow piece of plywood, measuring three or four inches in width by six or

Fig. 1   The Hungarian Weave

eight inches in length, makes a suitable loom for an attractive belt or strap. These bands of material are effective when used as straps for luggage racks, or they may be used as braid trimmings on costumes, as skirt bands, or as pockets for aprons.

A loom eight to ten inches square may be used for weaving material for hand bags. These pieces of cloth, fringed at one end, also may be used for mats.

Hungarian weaving makes a very attractive bath rug. For this purpose, it should be woven on a large plywood loom, with heavy cotton roving about one-fourth inch in diameter. Pleasing combinations of three or four colors may be worked out, such as: brown with tan, orange, and yellow; and black with red, gray, and white. Monochromatic tones of one color are effective, such as pink with rose; and deep rose with maroon.

When two colors are looped around one nail, the vertical rows of weaving will show two colors alternating the length of the material. If two loops of the same color are placed around the nail, a stripe of solid color will result.

A good project for a beginner is making a bookmark or belt, Fig. 2. This rather short piece of weaving can be done quickly and the short lengths of thread are easy to handle. The same loom may be used for a belt, after the weaver has mastered the handling of the threads.

Make the loom from a piece of plywood three inches by six inches. The thickness of the wood should be at least one-fourth of an inch but not more than seven-eighths of an inch. Cut the piece accurately and smooth all surfaces with sandpaper, so that the threads will not stick to the wood. The loom may be waxed, shellacked, or varnished for a smoother surface.

Draw a straight line, one inch from one of the narrow sides of the board, completely across the loom. Along this line place five three-fourths-inch brads or finishing nails, spacing them one-half inch apart. Drive the nails into the board so they stand rigidly in place, but do not extend through the board. Up and down each long side of the loom, place six more nails, one-half inch from the edge. If the plywood is thin and the nails penetrate, small legs or blocks may be placed

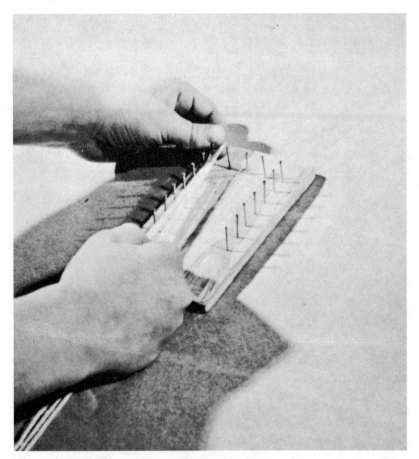

Fig. 2   Simple Loom for Hungarian Weaving

on the bottom to protect the table where the loom will be used. The loom is now ready to use to make a bookmark, belt, or for a longer length of band or strap.

Select soft cotton yarn, about one-eighth inch in diameter, of the type called cotton rug yarn. For the loom with five nails across the top, cut ten lengths of cotton yarn, each twenty-four inches long. The loom is threaded, or set up ready to weave, by looping two strands of yarn around each nail along the top of the loom. If three colors are chosen, arrange the loops of yarn so that the colors will lie across the surface of the loom in an

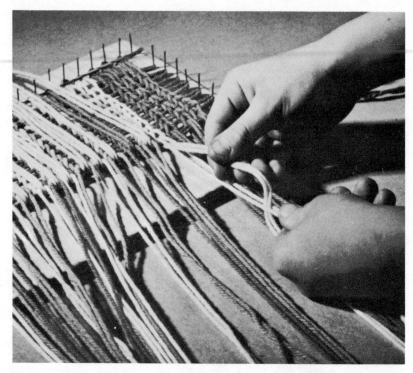

Fig. 3   Lower Threads Passed Through the Upper Layer in Pairs

orderly arrangement. One effective color scheme is black and red on the first and fifth nails, two red loops on the second and fourth nails, and a black loop and a white loop on the center nail. These are the warp threads or lengthwise threads and may be held in place flat on the loom by tying a cord around the loom or with rubber bands, just below the top row of nails.

The loom may be fastened to a table with a C-clamp if desired. Usually the weight of the plywood board is enough to keep the loom stable while weaving.

The weaving is done by separating the warp threads into *two layers*, Fig. 3. The weft thread passes between these layers.

Select the black threads on nails one and five, and place them straight up over the top of the loom. Select one pair of red threads from nails two and four, place them up over the loom, and place the black threads from nail three up over the top.

Placing the top layer of threads above the loom produces a shed through which the weaver or weft thread may pass. These threads hold their place in their layer all through the weaving.

A three-yard length of red from the same type of cotton yarn is used as a weaver in making the bookmark. The weaver, or weft thread is a double thread, so make a loop at the center of it and slip it over the first nail on the left hand side of the loom. Lay the weaver across the shed from left to right, close to the warp bend, and over the first nail on the right side of the loom. This is the first shot in the weaving.

Now for the Hungarian touch! The weaving, or braiding is done in pairs, Fig. 3. Each nail has two pairs of threads. Begin on the left side of the loom, and pick up the two black threads previously placed up over the loom; divide the two black threads; and reach through between them, to pick up the red

Fig. 4   "Weaver" Placed Across the Loom

pair looped around the same nail. Lay this red pair up over the loom. On nail two, bring down the previous pair with the left hand, reach through and bring through the first layer pair. Continue across the loom in this manner, until all five pairs which were previously up over the loom are brought down and the second layer of threads is in a row up over the loom.

When all the threads in the second layer have been brought up through pairs and have taken the position of the first layer, place the double thread weaver across the loom to the second nail on the left side of the loom, Fig. 4.

Proceed in this manner until the weaver has looped around the last nail. Then move the weaving up to the top of the loom. Loosen the ties or rubber bands and carefully slip the woven piece up over the nails. Move it up so the weaver loops around the first nail. The material is porous and can be easily pushed down over the top row of nails while the weaving continues.

The weaver may be spliced by tying on a new piece. The knot should be hidden in the shed so that it will not be noticed. When the Hungarian weaving is removed from the loom, all the loops around both sides and top may be chained together in a continuous chain, either with the fingers or with a large hook. The fourth side may be tied into a knotted fringe.

Many unusual and effective uses may be found for material woven in the Hungarian method. Long lengths of warp may be used for belts. Looms of greater width may be built to be used for the two sides of a knitting bag or shopping bag. Large looms, twenty-four to thirty inches in width and sixty inches in length, may be used for rug weaving. Heavy cotton roving makes a very effective rug, when many harmonizing colors are used.

One way to simplify Hungarian weaving is through the use of peg board with pegs and heavy threads. Tie just two pairs of warp threads around two pegs, and continue as above, using the pegs to hold the sides of the weft threads.

Some weavers prefer to use a nut pick and separate the warp threads in the braiding action after the weft threads have been laid across the loom.

Hungarian weaving lends itself to the use of many pleasing color combinations. Strong greens, such as a bright yellow-green combined with a dull moss green and woven across with a bright emerald green makes a handsome strap for a bag.

The loom is simple.

Materials are inexpensive.

The process is fascinating for nimble fingers.

It's fast.

It's fun.

Happy Hungarian Weaving!

CHAPTER 2

Weaving on a Hosiery Box

A cardboard box such as those used for packing ladies' hose may be easily made into a loom for weaving a piece of fabric approximately seven inches by ten inches. The rectangular mat has good proportion and lends itself to a variety of uses. One very practical use is a purse. The mat can be folded once, seamed on the edges, and a zipper can be attached across the top; or it can be folded into three sections, a loop worked in a buttonhole stitch, and a button attached.

Cotton carpet warp or heavy rug yarn make excellent warp or lengthwise threads, and a heavy rug yarn, sugar 'n cream yarn, or all-rayon Kentucky yarn, work up quickly and effectively when used as the weft, or cross threads.

A shuttle with a light color yarn may be used alternately with a thread of a dark color to produce vertical stripes.

One very effective color combination is brown carpet warp, with weft threads of brown, beige, and green Kentucky rayon yarn, alternating the colors the full length of the mat. Another combination might be warp of black yarn, with weft of red, gray, black, and white. Warp threads of a rich wine color pearl cotton #3 and weft colors of gray, rose, and wine heavy wool yarn are excellent choices.

The loom is quickly and easily constructed. A hosiery box, ruler, pins, and several small shuttles are all the equipment needed.

First, put the hosiery box in the lid to give the loom added strength. Then measure and mark with pencil divisions at one-

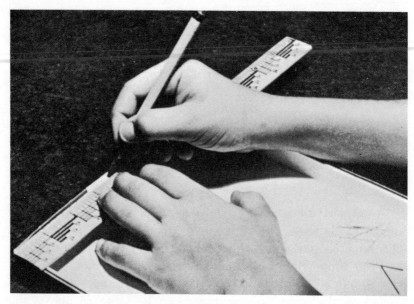

Fig. 5   Measuring the Hosiery Box

Fig. 6   Inserting Pins in the Hosiery Box

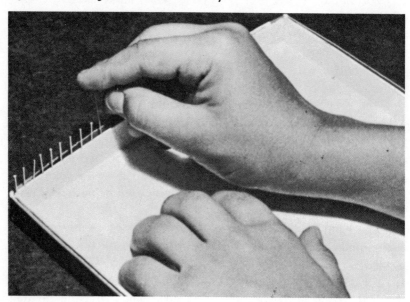

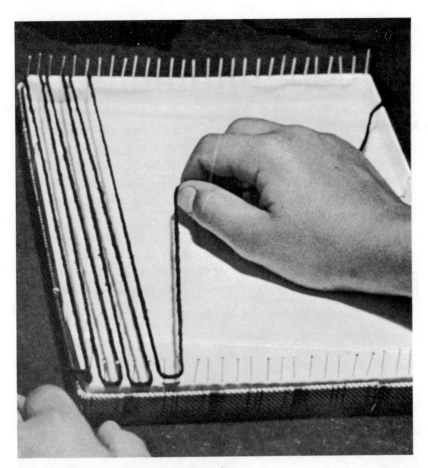

Fig. 7   Warping the Hosiery Box Loom

fourth of an inch intervals across each end of the box as shown
in Fig. 5.

Insert common pins at each mark so they stand vertically
and extend about one-half inch above the edge of the box as
shown in Fig. 6.

Select a colored carpet thread for warping the loom, and tie
the end securely to a corner pin. Wind across the loom, back
and forth from end to end, circling around two pins each time,
Fig. 7. These warp threads lie parallel, and equally spaced
along the loom. The threads should lie easily on the box, with-

out being stretched. Tie the warp thread around the last pin
and cut it off.

Make several thin shuttles, about three-fourths of an inch
wide and twelve inches long. These may be made of wood,
sanded smooth, or of heavy cardboard. Select the weft colors
and wind a color on each shuttle.

Begin to weave by laying the shuttle over the first thread,
under the second, over the third, under the fourth, etc., Fig. 8.
Pull the shuttle through the shed, but allow the end of the thread
to extend about two inches beyond the box. Turn this end around
the last thread and hide it by weaving over and under. This is
called *returning the end.*

Two shuttles may be used at the same time. Weave the
desired number of shots with one color; then use another color,
wound on a second shuttle, for the proper development of the
pattern. When using two colors and two shuttles, it is necessary

Fig. 8   Weaving on the Hosiery Box Loom

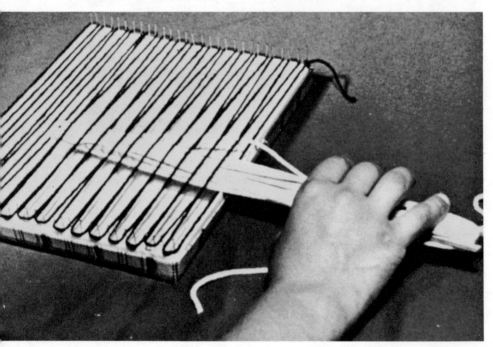

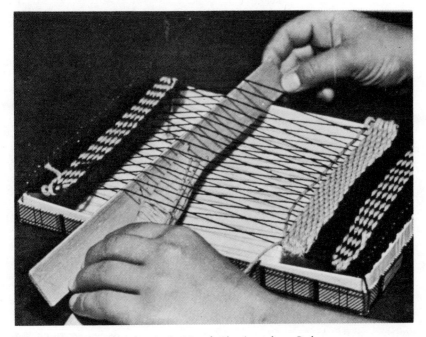

Fig. 9   Picking Up the Left-Hand Shed with a Ruler

to use extra care in turning the corner of the weft thread so that it lies very loosely, Fig. 9.

As the weaving progresses, any tendency for the selvage edges to draw in may be counteracted by pinning the woven cloth to the sides of the hosiery box.

When the color is changed in the weaving, the cut end should always be woven back into the cloth and clipped close to the surface, Fig. 10.

Figure 9 shows a method of speeding up the weaving. Most persons are more adept with the right hand, and can easily pick up alternate threads when weaving from right to left — under, over, under, over, etc. However, the left hand is usually a little clumsy, and a ruler inserted in the warp threads where the left-hand shots will be placed, is very helpful. It can be left in place, tilted slightly when needed, and the shuttle can be slid along the ruler, thus making the weaving from left to right much faster.

A heavy, wide-toothed comb is a good tool for beating the weft threads in place. However, the threads should not be packed down too closely, as the beauty of the individual threads should always be apparent in hand-woven material.

As the hosiery box loom is not too substantial, it helps to strengthen the weaving frame if both ends of the loom are used at the beginning of the weaving. For example, put in ten shots of a color at one end of the loom, then turn the loom and weave ten shots at the other end. This helps to hold the warp threads on the pins.

When the weaving has progressed so closely to the center of the loom that the shuttles have difficulty in picking up the threads, the balance of the mat may be finger-woven.

Remove the mat from the loom by removing pins from the box. Trim off ends and bits of threads from the surface of the mat as shown in Fig. 10.

Press under a damp cloth.

An interesting little purse may be made by lining the mat with a cloth of harmonizing color, inserting pieces of buckram

Fig. 10   Trimming Returned End of Weft Thread

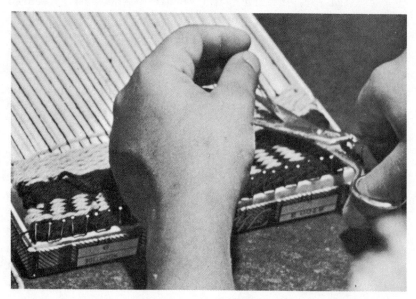

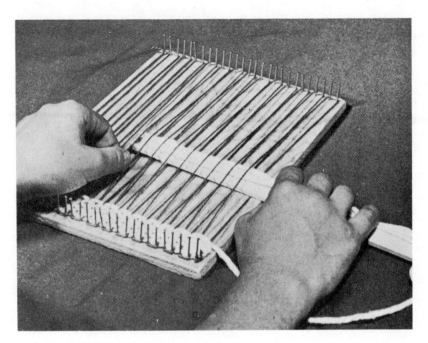

Fig. 11   Weaving on a Plywood Frame

or cardboard between the weaving and the lining, and folding the mat into an envelope shape with a flap.

The hosiery box is an excellent loom for making a little purse for evening wear, with bits of colored silk and gold threads woven into the cloth. Rough, nubby yarns add a textural interest.

A flat piece of plywood, seven inches by ten inches, makes a stronger loom, and is used the same way. Measure and cut the plywood board, smooth with sandpaper, and drive one-inch brads at each end. Place the nails at one-fourth of an inch intervals, and one-fourth of an inch from the ends of the board. Wind the warp threads and weave in the same way as on the hosiery box loom. Fig. 11 shows the plywood weaving frame, with the weaving started.

It is important to keep the pins at the ends of the hosiery box standing erect, and they should not be allowed to drop down into the cardboard during the weaving, as the warp threads might slip up over the pins.

The hosiery box makes a small delightful loom to carry about in a little larger box, and helps one become familiar with the terminology of weaving, such as the words warp, weft, parallel, shuttle, web, etc.

The small plywood loom shown in Fig. 11 makes an ideal sample loom to try such techniques as wrapped warps, tapestry weaving, inlay, and color changes of plaids and stripes.

CHAPTER 3

Finger Weaving

Finger weaving is a method of braiding or plaiting which produces a band or strap. The term finger weaving is very appropriate, for not even a shuttle is necessary. The warp, or lengthwise, threads are picked up one by one with the fingers and used as weft or cross threads.

This interlacing of harmonizing colors of heavy warp threads gives a woven band, the width of which is determined by the number and size of warp threads. These bands may be used as belts, cord-pulls, straps for luggage racks, bookmarks, or trimmings. Bands of finger weaving give a peasant touch when used around skirt hems, across pockets, or on aprons.

A twelve-inch piece of one-half inch dowel rod, or a large pencil is used to hold the warp threads. Tie a cord to the ends of the dowel rod, and loop the cord over a nail or hook.

The thread chosen for weaving depends upon the use to be made of the finished band, but a good material for learning the technique is a heavy cotton yarn, such as sugar 'n cream yarn or a lightweight rug yarn. Choose three or four colors which, when combined, will give the desired effect — either the bold contrast of such colors as brilliant red with black and gray, or possibly the more subtle color combination of violet, fuchia, and light pink. Cut nine or twelve lengths of yarn, depending upon the width of belt or strap desired. Each piece should be four yards long if a belt is to be made. Arrange the yarn on the dowel rod for weaving with strands of the same color together to produce a simple zig-zag design. Since the

strands form the weft threads as well as the warp, the colors
should be carefully planned.

The snitch knot, Fig. 12, is made by taking the center of
the four-yard strand, placing it over the rod, and drawing the
two ends through. Fasten each thread on the dowel with a
snitch knot, placing them in the desired order.

If nine strands were used, you now have eighteen ends
hanging from the dowel, each two yards long, and the colors
are grouped together. These colors will zig-zag back and forth
across the belt as the weaving is done. The belt will not be the
length of the strands, for they are the warp *and* weft threads.

Now for the weaving! Pick up the first thread on the right
side and carry it over the second thread, under the third, etc.,
continuing over and under across the band from right to left.

Fig. 12   The Snitch Knot

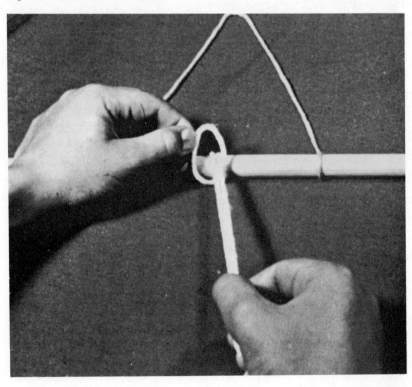

Pull it out at the left side and drape the end up over the rod, where it will hang until needed, Fig. 13.

Weave the next thread from the right side over and under, toward the left hand selvage in the same manner. When this weaver reaches the edge, bring down the first thread that was draped up over the rod and replace it with the second thread. Draping the last weaver or weft up on the rod makes the path of the weft thread very definite.

Proceed to weave the entire belt in this way, always using the thread on the right side. The bands of colors will move

Fig. 13   Weaving Across the Belt

Fig. 14   The Guatemalan Method of Finishing Ends

from side to side across the belt. Keep the selvage turns loose
and easy. The fingers *place* the threads.

When the threads are too short to weave, the end may
be finished off in one of several ways. Boys' belts should be
firmly stitched by sewing machine into a pointed shape. The
dowel rod should be drawn out of the loops and the loops tied
to a buckle.

The Guatemalan method of tiny braids is an interesting
finish for girls' belts. Pick up the three threads on the left and
braid to the ends. Braid the other strands in sets of three
threads. Press under a damp cloth to hold the ends in place,
Fig. 14.

Another method of placing the colors on the rod produces
the chevron pattern. For this pattern, place equal strands of
matching colors on each side, then a like number of strands of

the next color on the inside of the first color, and a center section of the same width. For example, the threading might be, from right to left, two black strands, two red strands, two white strands, two red strands, and two black strands. (Ten in all.)

Figure 15 shows a bookmark being woven in the chevron design, with a pencil used as the rod.

To weave the chevron pattern, begin in the center of the group and weave the center right strand to the left. Then take the center left strand and weave it over to the right side of the band. The selvages are turned the same way as in the zig-zag weaving. Place the weft up over the end of the dowel until the new weft thread takes its place.

When using bands of finger-woven material for trimming, stitch the ends securely into a seam of the garment.

Fig. 15   Weaving the Chevron Pattern

Finger-woven bands of heavy wool, four-ply knitting worsted yarn in shades of golden brown, chartreuse, and beige would make a striking decoration for a brown velveteen bag.

Another striking use of finger weaving results when the colors are woven as a group instead of as individual threads. . . . For instance, the threads may be placed on the pencil in such colors as four threads of copper, four threads of orange, four threads of caramel tan, four threads of warm brown, and then the weaving done with the four strands used together as one strand.

Long, long strands of warps might be wound on small shuttles for easier handling, or might be chained as a warp chain to shorten the length at the beginning of the braid.

The possibilities for unusual effects in finger weaving with nubby and metallic yarns and threads are unlimited.

CHAPTER 4

Spool Weaving

Spool weaving is an old method of making a round flexible cord. The size of coil desired and the type of thread to be used determine the size of loom necessary. A very fine thread, such as pearl cotton #3 may be used on an empty spool. Heavy rug

Fig. 16   Beginning to Weave on the Spool Loom

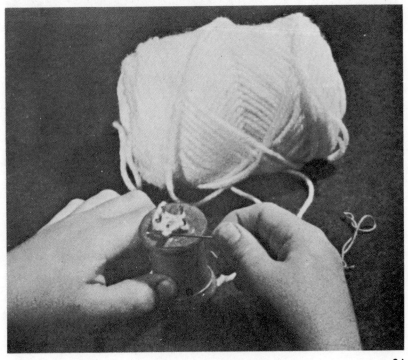

yarn makes a coil about an inch in diameter and requires a loom large enough to accommodate this size.

To make a simple loom for small threads, secure a common wooden spool, about the size used for #8 sewing thread, Fig. 16. Drive five small nails or wire brads around the top of the spool-hole, spacing them equally around the hole and far enough away from it to avoid splitting the spool. The use of five nails instead of the more common four gives a more interesting coil and makes it easier to hide the sewing of the finished coil.

The nails should extend one-half inch or slightly higher above the spool. A wool yarn or #3 cotton is suitable for weaving a small round mat for one side of a coin purse, or for use as a round pot holder. Insert the end of the yarn through

Fig. 17   Sanding the Spool Loom

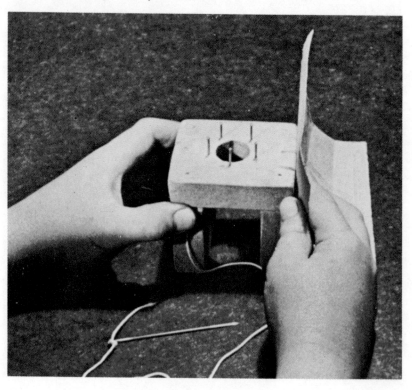

Fig. 18   Boring the Hole for a Spool Loom

the spool and wrap the yarn to the left. Pass the thread around
a nail, then skip a nail, around a nail, then skip a nail. Continue
until all the nails have a loop of yarn around them, Fig. 20.

This method of threading produces a star shape when the
spool is ready for weaving.

Use a large darning needle or long thin nail for a pick.
The needle may be tied to the spool, to keep it from being lost.
Notice the string in Fig. 17.

Now turn the spool, allowing the yarn to make a second
loop on the first nail. As this second row of yarn is placed on
each nail, lift the lower loop up, out, and over the top of the
nail, leaving only the new loop of yarn on the nail. Continue
around the spool, lifting off the *lower loop* with the sharp point
of the weaving needle. Be sure to get the lower loop firmly on
the needle, then pull it up, out and over the top of the nail. Keep
the loops rather loose as the weaving progresses, so that the
finished coil will be smooth and easy to handle. The coil develops
and grows down through the hole in the spool.

When a coil of a larger diameter is desired, it is easy to make a loom of soft white pine. About the only tools required are: a suitable auger bit, a brace, a clamp or vise, a pencil, a ruler, a coping saw, and a hammer and nails.

Make a little flat table with top about three inches square, and two legs of the same wood measuring two inches by three inches. Soft white pine three-quarters of an inch thick makes a sturdy loom, Fig. 18.

Secure a suitable piece of wood, sand it smooth, and lay out the three pieces. On the square top draw diagonal lines with the ruler and pencil. Where they cross, bore a one-half inch hole. Fig. 19 shows an easy way to measure the top and end pieces before sawing.

Fig. 19   Cutting the Spool Loom

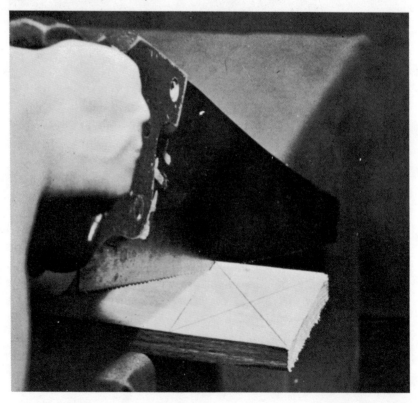

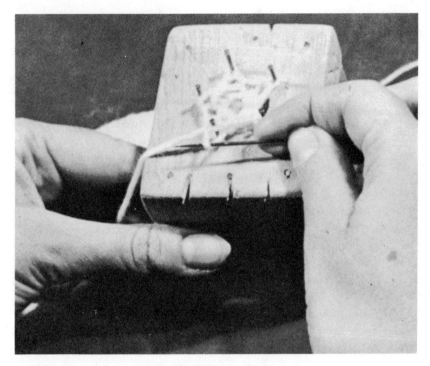

Fig. 20 Threading a Spool Loom

Make pencil dots to locate the five finishing nails or wire brads around the hole. The nails should be spaced evenly and about one-half inch from the hole. Drive the nails into the wood until they extend one-half inch above the surface.

Nail the sides or legs to the top. A round file will smooth the sides of the hole and make the coil slip down through the hole easily. Sand the rough edges of the loom. A little table loom of this type puts the weaving up where it can be more easily seen. The loom with the half-inch hole may be used with 4-ply knitting worsted wool yarn as shown in Fig. 20. The coil will grow rapidly as weaving progresses.

A loom with a hole $\frac{3}{4}''$ to $1\frac{1}{4}''$ in diameter may be used for a coil of rug yarn. If a bit this large is not available, bore a hole as large as possible, insert a coping saw blade, and saw a hole of the desired size. This loom would require a larger piece of soft pine for the table. The weaving is done in exactly the same manner.

The sewing of the mat may begin as soon as the coil is about eighteen inches long. Use a large needle with thread or string of matching color, or sew with the same material as used to make the coil. Sew or lace the coils together around and around, picking up with the needle one stitch on each of the two adjacent coils. Hold the coils flat in a circle or oval while sewing or lacing, Fig. 21.

For a pot holder, use cotton rug yarn in colors suitable for kitchen use. Tie the ends together when changing colors and push the knot into the center of the coil. When the mat reaches a diameter of five inches, cut the thread, draw the end through all five loops, and sew the end down flat. A small white bone ring may be attached to the edge for a hanger.

A small coin purse may be woven of two round mats of 4-ply knitting worsted wool. Choose harmonious colors and attach a small zipper halfway around the edges. A lining is not necessary for a coin purse of spool woven coil. After attaching the zipper, sew the rest of the way around the circle.

The spool-woven cord makes an excellent jumping rope when made of strong cotton carpet warp. Slip the ends of the rope through gaily painted large spools for handles. Hold the handles of the jumping rope in place with knots in the cord.

The coil makes an attractive belt for a bath robe. It may also be used as a three-dimensional fashion touch for a girl's flaring skating skirt. One attractive way is to tack it around the edge in loops or scallops.

Fig. 22 shows how the larger size table loom makes a fine heavy cord for a rug. Notice that a strong hook makes a better weaver or pick for the rug yarn. When lacing the coil together, wind it loosely on a flat surface so that the finished rug will lie flat on the floor.

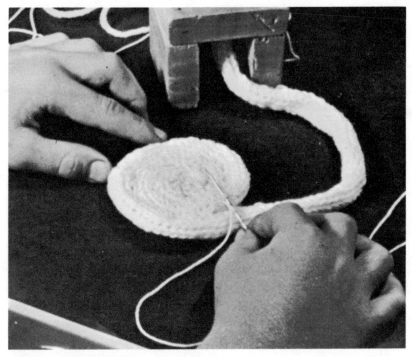

Fig. 21   Sewing Spool-Woven Coil

Fig. 22   Spool Weaving Loom for a Rug Coil

CHAPTER 5

The Slot Loom

The slot loom, sometimes called a knitting rake, is a simple wooden loom which produces a flat length of fabric very similar to a knitted cloth. The loom may be used to produce tubular cloth, or by more intricate threading, various other weaves and textures. Only one simple method of weaving will be discussed here.

The slot loom can be made any width desired. It can be large enough to weave a head scarf thirty-six inches square

Fig. 23   Driving Nails in the Slot Loom

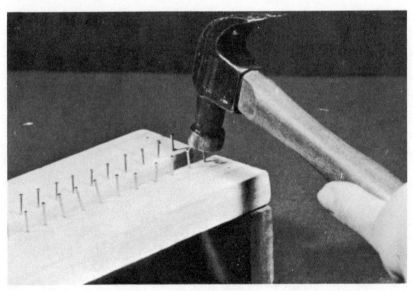

but for most uses a shorter loom will be found more practical. A loom twelve inches long will produce a fabric wide enough for a scarf.

Select a good piece of white pine and cut two pieces 2″ x 12″ and two pieces 2″ x 2½″. Fasten the two long boards to the smaller pieces as shown in Fig. 23. These short legs make it more convenient to use the loom, and keeps the weaving up where the weaver can see the progress of the web. The top long boards should be fastened on the legs so they are one-half inch apart. The hole or slot between the top boards gives the loom its name. Place pencil marks along the edge of each of the top boards, one-half inch apart and about one-eighth of an inch from the inside edge. Drive a small wire brad into the loom at each point, allowing them to extend about one-half inch, Fig. 23.

For a wool scarf, select heavy, four-ply knitting worsted wool in a color which will harmonize with a winter coat.

Tie the end of the yarn to the first nail, then loop it around the first nail on the other side of the slot, bringing the yarn back across the slot and around the second nail. Continue this threading down the loom for as great a distance as the width of the fabric, Fig. 24.

Turn around the last nail and put another layer of yarn on the *same nails* used on the first threading. The yarn should not be stretched, as it may slide up off the nails. It will stay in place after the first row is woven off. It is important that the yarn be looped over the same nails on each threading. The loom is threaded, then woven, then threaded again, then woven, etc.

With a large darning needle (fastened to the loom with a string so it will not be lost), lift the lower loop up, out and over the nail; then proceed to the next nail and loop the lower yarn up, out and over the nail. Finish one side and then weave off the other side. This weaving process is the same as in spool weaving. Again thread the loom by laying a layer of yarn on the same nails used before. Weave off. The end nail in each layer is used for turning and cannot be woven off each row.

An interesting effect of stripes appears when two colors are used. Thread the loom and weave two threadings of the first

Fig. 24 Threading the Slot Loom

color. Tie on the second color and weave off two threadings; then use the first color again for two threadings, etc. Do not cut the yarn off, as the thread may be picked up and used again after two threadings of the second color. The ends of the wool yarn are always on the same side of the loom. Fig. 24 shows the threading process and also the finished weave of the scarf as it grows down through the slot. It is very important to keep the loops rather loose on the nails. This makes for faster weaving and produces a more uniform weave.

When the scarf is the desired length, usually about thirty inches long, it may be finished in any of several ways. One way is to pull the loops up through the slot, pick up the first loop with a large #4 bone hook, pulling the second through it.

Then pull the third loop through the second, etc. Proceed across the end of the scarf, pulling the end of the yarn through the last loop. Fig. 25 shows the hook being used to finish the end of a scarf.

Another method is to hook the end of the yarn through every loop on the end of the scarf. Cut the yarn from the ball and hide the raw end of the thread.

An interesting finish for a scarf is a two-color fringe cut and tied in. Cut eight-inch lengths of two colors of yarn. Pick up one of each of the two colors, fold in the center, and pull this loop through the first stitch in the end of the scarf, Fig. 26. Pull the four yarn ends through the loop. Continue across the two ends of the scarf.

To block the scarf to shape, dip in cool water, pat into shape on a table, and allow to dry.

Fig. 25 Finishing Off the Scarf

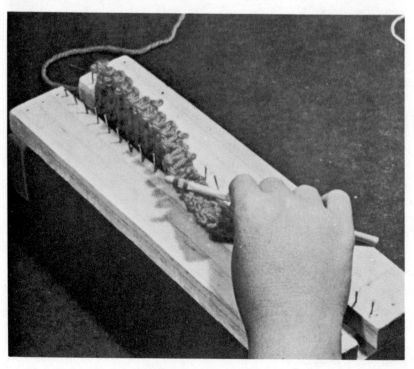

Fig. 26   Tying in Fringe on the Scarf

CHAPTER 6

The T-D Loom

The T-D loom, a simple loom for weaving narrow fabric, is made from tongue-depressor blades. The loom is rather limiting to the weaver, as it produces strips of cloth only five or six inches in width; but it is so inexpensive to build and so much fun to use that everyone should try weaving on a T-D loom. A belt woven on the T-D loom makes a good beginning weaving project.

Fig. 27 Laying Out Center Holes in Tongue Depressers

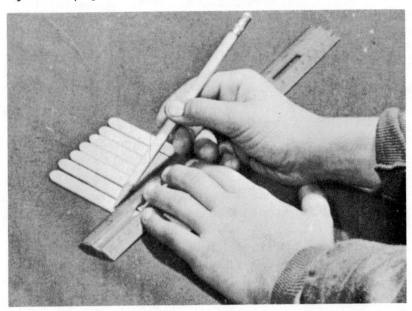

The loom is a heddle frame which is raised and lowered to form the two weaving sheds. Use seven tongue depressors for the frame. Find the exact centers of each blade, and bore a one-eighth inch hole at that point, Fig. 27. Make a similar hole in each end. Place two more tongue depressers on the table, as far apart as their length. Arrange the first seven tongue depressers side by side on these two blades. They should be close together, but there should be room for a thread of #3 pearl cotton to slide up and down between the blades. Mark through the end holes of the blades and then bore the seven holes in the top and bottom cross bars.

Drill identical holes in two more blades so the loom can be wired together at the top and bottom. Fig. 28 shows the threading of the T-D loom. The use of a cross blade on both sides of the heddle frame makes the frame stronger. The loom is lifted up or pushed down to open a shed for the shuttle to pass through. The spacing of the blades along the horizontal top and bottom blades is very important. Just enough space should be allowed between blades for the thread to slip up and down easily.

Attach the seven horizontal blades to the top and lower braces with wire. The seven blades placed in a vertical position are held there by four more blades, two at the top and two at the bottom, firmly wired together. This size T-D loom will carry 15 warp threads.

Make several shuttles from T-D blades by cutting notches in each end.

Two pieces of flat thin wood or dowel rod are needed to hold the warp taut. Cut two six-inch lengths. Fasten a strong cord on both ends of each dowel. The cord on one rod should be long enough to encircle the waist of the weaver. The warp threads are tied on one dowel, threaded through the heddles and slots, and tied on the second dowel which is fastened around the weaver's waist.

Select #3 pearl cotton, carpet warp, or rug yarn in the desired color for the warp threads. These may be all the same color or two alternating colors. Cut 15 threads, each two yards long. Tie the first thread securely around the dowel and bring

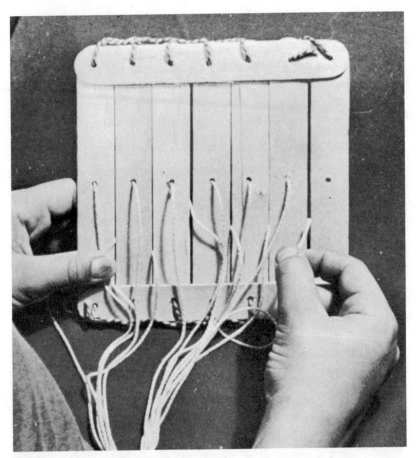

Fig. 28   Threading the T-D Loom

it down on the outside edge of the heddle frame, Fig. 28. Tie
the second thread to the dowel and bring it down through the
first T-D blade hole. Pass the third thread between the first two
blades. Continue to thread the loom, passing one thread through
a blade, one through the slot between, one through the blade, etc.

Loop the cord on the dowel around a door-knob or clamp
the dowel to a table. Bring all the ends firmly down through
the frame toward the weaver and tie them around the second
dowel, which is fastened around the weaver's waist. The warp
threads should be smooth and taut from one dowel to the other.

A strong linen cord tying the warp threads to a door-knob,
table leg, or any stationary piece of furniture helps hold the
warp threads taut. Sometimes the loom can be tied between two
chairs. . . . in fact, any method of holding the threads taut is fine.

Wind shuttles with harmonizing colors of very heavy cotton
or wool yarn. Strips of cotton cloth one inch wide may be woven
in at the very beginning to help space the warp threads. The

Fig. 29   Raising the T-D Loom to Open the Shed

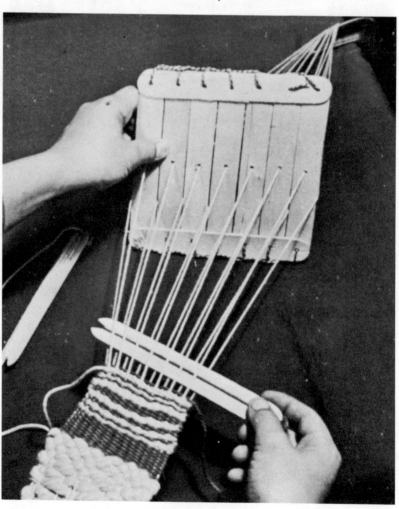

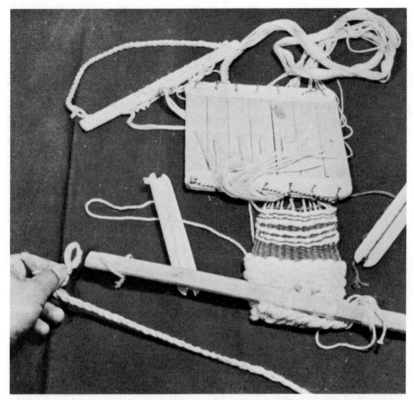

Fig. 30   Cord Encircles Weaver's Waist and Attaches to Front Beam

heddle frame should be kept at a comfortable distance from the weaver.

Hold the shuttle in the right hand, lean back on the warp to tighten it, and pull straight up on the T-D heddle frame with the left hand. This brings up all the threads which pass through the blades and opens a shed for the shuttle. Pass the shuttle from right to left. For the next shot, press down on the heddle frame, pushing down all the threads which pass through the blades, and opening the opposite shed for passing the shuttle from left to right.

A coarse-tooth comb may be used for beating the weft threads into place. Several shots across the loom will be required before the web begins to develop.

Stripes of varied width give an interesting effect. A belt of
red, black, and white Kentucky rayon yarn makes a colorful
accent for a white summer dress. The ends of new threads are
returned and overlapped in the same way as in most other
methods of weaving.

When the web grows too long for the weaver to reach the
heddle frame comfortably, the web or woven cloth may be rolled
up on the front dowel and pinned securely in place.

Figure 30 shows the heddle frame and end dowels complete
with cords.

Most weaving techniques may be worked out on the T-D
loom, and may include the inlay with separate shuttles as shown
in Fig. 31. When the woven fabric is finished and the entire warp

Fig. 31   Trimming Surface of T-D Weaving

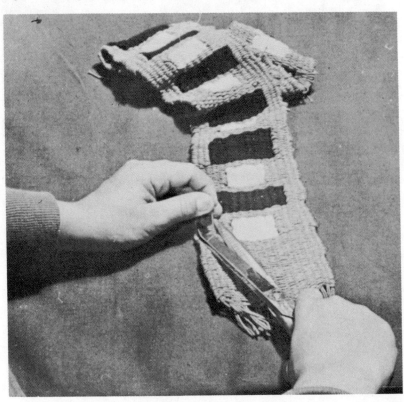

has been used, cut the warp ends loose from the dowel rods and tie together in groups of two. One end of the belt may be sewn into a point and a buckle attached to the other end. Strips of T-D weaving may be joined and used as a purse or for trimming skirts or costumes. There is something very primitive and satisfying about the weaving on a T-D loom. The Indians kept the warp threads taut by tying them to a tree.

CHAPTER 7

Waffle Weaving

The waffle loom is a small wood frame, usually ten inches square. The fabric is a three-dimensional cloth with the warp and weft threads tied or bound together at the corners where they intersect. It is suitable for a hot dish mat for the table. A very good place mat may be made on a frame whose outside dimensions are thirteen by nineteen inches.

A soft-twist cotton makes a sponge-like mat when it is removed from the frame. The many layers of thread make a soft thick mat, fringed on all four sides.

The frame may be made of one-fourth-inch plywood. Cut four 1″ x 10″ pieces and fasten them together with a miter joint. Drive three-fourths-inch finishing nails or wire brads all around the outside, at intervals of one-fourth of an inch.

The loom pictured in Fig. 32 is a commercial model which is made with grooved slots around the edge.

The mat may be woven with white thread throughout or colors may be used to produce borders or plaid effects.

Warping and tying in waffle weaving is very simple. Tie the end of a spool of #3 pearl cotton thread at one corner of the frame. Wind the thread eight times around each nail or groove, before proceeding to the next groove where again eight rounds are wound on. After all the vertical threads are in place, turn across the corner, and wind the loom horizontally, Fig. 32. When eight rounds have been placed on each nail, in each direction, the threading is completed. Tie the thread at the last corner.

At one corner of the frame tie a thread of the color desired for the knots. This thread should be about two yards long so it

53

Fig. 32   Winding Warp for Waffle Weaving

will be easy to handle. Two knots are tied at each intersection and on the wrong side of the mat. Viewed from the right side each little intersection has a cross thread, making a neat little X. These knots hold the cloth together.

After tying the thread at the corner of the frame, bring the thread out to the first intersection of the vertical and horizontal threads. Pass the thread across the intersection, push it down through the underside, bring it up across the corner and through a loop held up in a twist. This knot tightens around the threads like a lasso. Then tie another knot in the same place, but crossing diagonally in the opposite direction. These lasso knots may be tied diagonally across the mat from corner to corner, as shown in Fig. 33; or they may be tied in straight lines around the edge of the loom.

If a contrasting color of thread is used for tying and the knots are tied from corner to corner diagonally across the mat, the web of crosses which will appear on the underneath side of the mat will add an interesting design.

Fig. 34 shows a mat made of white, yellow, and beige #3 pearl cotton, wound on the frame to make a plaid design, and tied with orange. An unusual color scheme would be to tie the

Fig. 33   Tying the Loop Knot

groups of threads individually, changing color at various points to form a design.

An interesting color combination might be royal blue, outside border, delft blue just inside the edge of the royal blue, then a group on all four sides of medium blue, with the center finished with groups of very pale blue. This mat could be tied with the royal blue.

To remove the mat from the frame, slide a single edge razor blade around the edge of the frame. Trim the finished mat to remove unwanted surface threads and trim the sides of the fringed border.

Fig. 34   Tightening the Knot

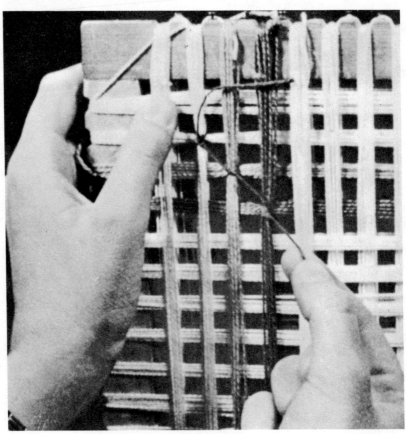

CHAPTER 8

Weaving on the Flat Loom

The flat loom is easy to use, sturdily constructed, and inexpensive. Most makes are adjustable to various sizes. It is an excellent loom for mastering the simple over and under technique and may be used by very young children. The warp threads are set at one-fourth inch intervals. One very important feature of some flat looms are metal bars which fit into holes at the ends of the loom and hold the selvages straight. Many times the beginning weaver is disappointed in his mat because the edges have pulled in, giving an hourglass appearance. By using the wire rod as part of the warp, the edges are held straight.

Many types of thread may be used on the flat loom. Cotton warps of 10/2 with weft of Kentucky rayon are effective and an all wool mat made of four-ply knitting worsted yarn for both warp and weft is attractive.

To warp the loom, tie the end of a spool of warp around one of the wire rods at the bent end. Place the first thread right on top of the wire rod, take it across the loom and thread it through the first slot, then back through the second slot and so on across the loom, Fig. 35. Allow the last thread to lie on top of the other wire rod. Adjust this rod in the loom so the end of the thread can be tied around the bent end of the rod. Note that a continuous warp thread is wound back and forth across the loom. The outside warp threads are used simultaneously with the wire rod.

Select a coarse thread for the weft. Thread the flat needle-like shuttle or use a very narrow, twelve-inch regulation shuttle.

Weave under, over, etc., from the right-hand side of the loom, Fig. 36. Allow a two-inch end of the weft thread to hang at the selvage; then with the fingers turn this end and weave it under and over to hide it in the web of weaving. Now insert a ruler on the opposite tabby, (over and under). When weaving from the left side of the loom, turn the ruler on edge in the warp and slide the shuttle along the ruler, pulling the weft thread through the shed. This method of using the ruler and allowing it to remain in the warp while weaving does away with awkward motions in picking up threads when weaving from the left.

The weaver will find that returning ends, joining new threads, striping, inlay, and other techniques may be very easily employed when weaving on the flat loom. One of the most effective unusual effects is to weave in loops of heavy wool. This decorative weaving gives a three-dimensional effect to the surface and is easy to do, requiring only a pair of wooden knitting needles, Fig. 37.

Fig. 35   Threading the Flat Loom

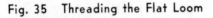

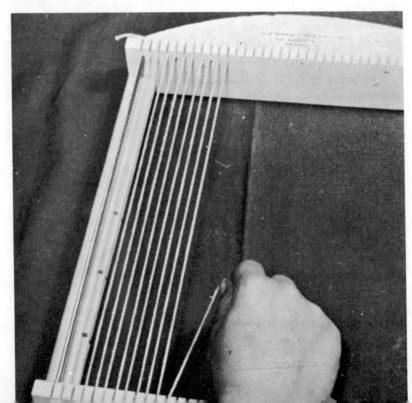

The loops are twisted around the knitting needle when the right to left thread lies loosely in the shed. The weft is pulled up over the tip of the needle at intervals all across the mat, Fig. 37. Weave plain weave back from left to right. After several rows have been woven, the knitting needle may be twisted out, leaving a neat little row of loops. Two rows of loops, close together may be woven in by using the pair of needles.

Fig. 36   Picking Up Threads on the Flat Loom

Fig. 38 shows the knitting needle being removed when several rows of plain weave have been completed. Designs and figures may be worked out in this same loop technique, with the background in plain color and the loops in matching or harmonizing color.

The ruler may be used for weaving from left to right until the space becomes too narrow to insert the shuttle. Then the balance of the weaving must be finished by weaving with the fingers.

Fig. 37   Loop Weaving on the Flat Loom

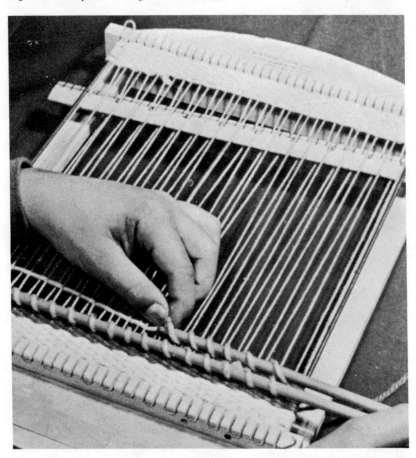

Notice in Fig. 38 that the ruler stays in the shed. The weft thread travels around the edge thread and rod together. Be sure the shuttle never separates the side thread from the rod. The use of the rod helps to keep straight sides or selvages.

When the weaving is finished, the loops of warp may be pulled up away from the loom, the rods pulled out and the finished mat trimmed of surface threads. The mat makes a very attractive table mat or it may be folded and sewed to make a purse. Fringe may be tied to the ends if desired.

Fig 38   Removing Knitting Needle

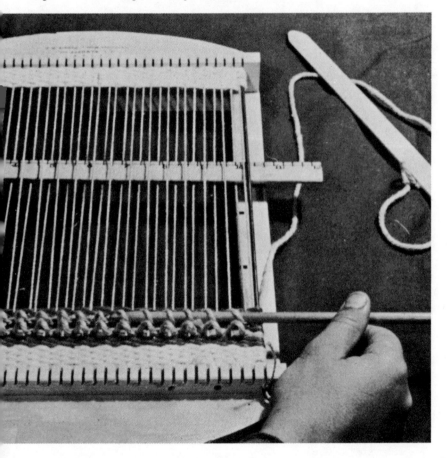

CHAPTER 9

Card Weaving

Card weaving is a type of true weaving, with warp threads running lengthwise, and weft threads running through the warp threads. The weft thread may be wound on a shuttle, or used directly from a small ball. The weaving is done with a number of heavy cardboard cards, three inches square with a hole in each corner one-fourth of an inch in diameter. Sets of cards for Egyptian card weaving may be purchased, or cards may be cut with litttle difficulty.

When handmade cards are used the corner weaving holes are placed about three-fourths of an inch from the rounded corner. Draw diagonal lines and place the four holes on the lines. Six cards may be clamped together, the corners sanded into an easy curve, and the holes drilled in all the cards at the same time, using a one-fourth-inch bit. This method assures that all holes are in line.

Card weaving is a very ancient art; evidence of it has been found in old Egyptian tombs. American Indians knew the craft, too, as pieces of flat shell with four corner holes have been found among Indian relics.

Card weaving produces a band or strap which is remarkably strong and suitable for belts, luggage racks, bag handles, etc., where a well-made decorative band is needed. Very elaborate designs are possible and books have been written on its possibilities and patterns, with as many as thirty-two cards. The method of weaving with six cards will be described in detail. More elaborate aesigns are possible with more cards.

After the cards have been cut from cardboard and the holes drilled, number the cards from one to six. Mark the four holes in a clockwise manner, starting with *A* in the upper left-hand corner, *B* should be in the upper right-hand corner, *C* in the lower right-hand corner, and *D* in the lower left-hand corner. The commercial cards are printed in this manner.

Select four colors of #3 pearl cotton or 4-ply knitting worsted wool and make a diagram of threading according to the colors selected. Suggested colors for a belt might be black, white, red, and gray; brown, tan, orange, and green; or violet, rose, pink, and natural.

To make the color threading diagram, number like this to represent the six cards:

1	2	3	4	5	6

Down the left side, write the letters *A*, *B*, *C*, and *D* to represent the holes in each card:

	1	2	3	4	5	6
A						
B						
C						
D						

A good design of color spacing is to have cards one and six alike, cards two and five alike, and cards three and four alike. If black, white, gray and red were selected, the diagram would be:

	1	2	3	4	5	6
A	B	B	R	R	B	B
B	W	R	B	B	R	W
C	R	W	R	R	W	R
D	G	G	W	W	G	G

B means black, G means gray, W means white, R means red.

Check the diagram to be sure the sides of the design are the same in color placement, if the edges of the woven strip are to be the same.

Draw a dotted line down the center of the diagram as a warning to help in the threading.

When the cards and threading diagram are complete, begin the threading with card *1*. All threads should be three yards long for a belt. To thread the first card, put through the hole marked *A* the color designated as *A* on the diagram. In the threading diagram given here, the first card shows black in

Fig. 39   Threading Card One

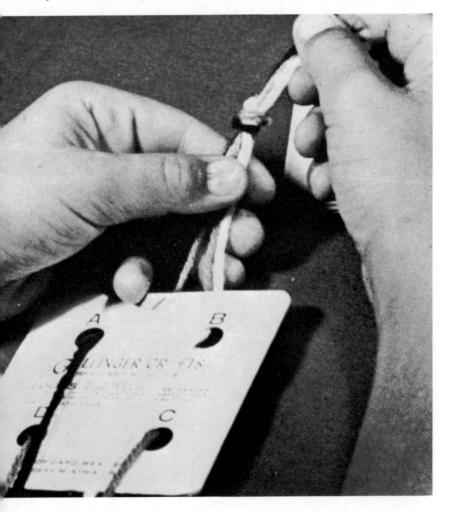

A, white in *B*, red in *C* and gray in *D*. Put these four threads through the front of the card and tie them all together in a knot at the back of the card. Fig. 39 shows card *1* threaded and the knot being tied. Now thread card *2* with black, red, white and gray, as designated on the diagram. Fig. 40 shows card *2* being threaded. Tie the threads together at the back of the card and place on top of card *1*. Thread card *3* according to the diagram. Place the card on the number *1* and *2* cards already threaded. The balance of the cards, or the right-hand side of the diagram are all threaded by bringing the ends of the threads through from the back of the card instead of through the front, Fig. 41. The knots are tied on each card the same way and the cards are stacked together, with the knots extending above the pack of six cards. Changing the threading direction is necessary to assure a symmetrical pattern in the belt.

Fig. 40   Threading Card Two

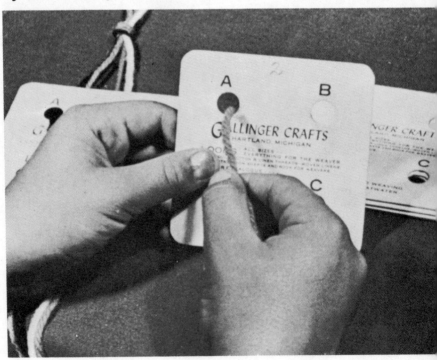

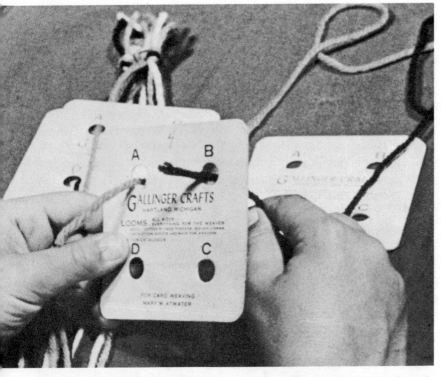

Fig. 41   Cards are Threaded from Back on Right Side of Belt Threads

Loop a strong cord through all the six knots and tie it securely. Fasten to a table with a clamp or tie to a suitable and convenient holder. Pull all the cards, held carefully together, down the length of the warp threads. Smooth and straighten all twenty-four threads until they are taut. Then tie the free ends together. Knot a strong cord to this end of the threads and tie to the weaver's belt, or around the waist. Then by leaning back the warp threads can be tightened. Move the pack of six cards to within twelve inches of the weaver, or a comfortable reaching distance. Check the cards to see that all *A* corners match, all cards are face up and all *A* corners are on top and toward the weaver. The shed opens in the center side of the card. Choose a weft color, preferably one of the colors which has been used in the warp, and lay the end in the shed. Fig. 42

shows cards correctly held in *A* position, ready to insert the weft thread.

Turn all the cards together at once until the *B* corner is up and toward the weaver. A new shed is opened. Insert the weft thread in the new shed. Then turn all cards together until the *C* corner is up and toward the weaver. Insert the weft thread. Turn all the cards back to the *B* corner and insert the weft thread. This rotation of cards, *A,B,C,B,* repeated over and over, will not twist the warp threads and will produce a repeated pattern throughout the length of the belt. The weft thread travels back and forth across the belt in true weft fashion.

Fig. 42   Opening the Shed

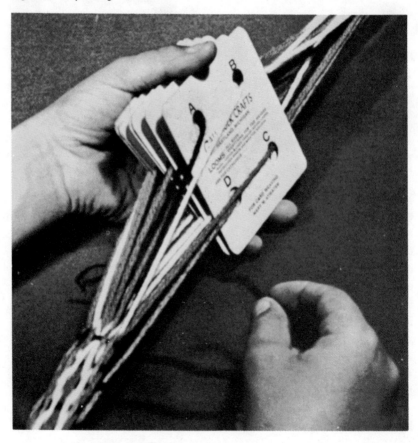

Fig. 43 shows the cards being turned into the *B* position. Sometimes it may be necessary to help the shed to open neatly with the fingers. A weft thread of the same color as the edge of the belt is less noticeable on the selvage. The tightness of the weft determines to a large extent the width of the belt. A ruler may be used to pack the weft threads in place.

Sometimes loops of weft are left on the selvage edges for decoration. .

As the weaving progresses it will be necessary to get closer to the work. The heavy cord may be loosened and the knot moved up on the woven strap, then re-tied around the waist.

Fig. 43   Turning the Pack of Cards

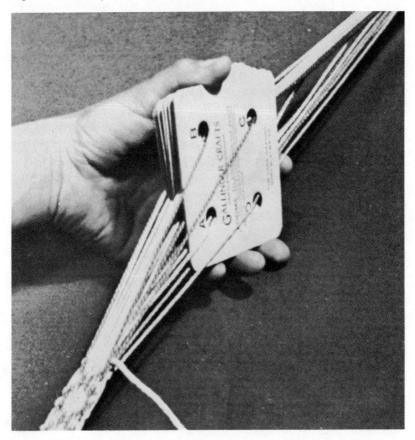

When leaving the weaving it is suggested that a complete pattern be rotated, *A,B,C,B,* so that it will be easy to begin the weaving without interruption of the pattern.

When the weaving is completed, the first knots are untied, the cards slipped off the warp threads, and the ends knotted together, or machine stitched, as desired. Sewing is best for a boy's belt. The cards may be used over and over.

After weaving with six cards is mastered, an interested weaver would enjoy trying many more cards, even as many as thirty-two. The method is the same. The pattern diagram should be symmetrical, and the threading should be through the front of the cards to the center of the diagram, then through the back of the cards for the right-hand side of the belt.

A simplified method of card weaving is done by cutting four or more cards from heavy corrugated cardboard similar to a packing case. Cut the cards about $1\frac{1}{2}''$ x 6″ and with a large paper punch, punch a hole in the exact center of each card.

This card weaving can be done rather like the inkle weaving, with a thread through each hole and a thread not in a card, but just stretched between the cards. Try tying five brown threads of heavy carpet wool, and four beige threads together in a large knot at the end. Tie the knot to a stationary object. Then thread the beige threads through the cards, one to each of the four cards. Arrange the brown threads at the beginning and the end, or on both sides of the group, and also one between each card. When the threads are taut, cut a small cardboard shuttle and wind with the brown heavy thread.

The two sheds are produced by raising and lowering the cards in a group, allowing the beige threads in the cards to be first above, and then below the brown warp threads.

The shuttle then passes through the alternate sheds, first right, then left, and the resulting web can be used for a belt, or a headband, or a bracelet.

CHAPTER 10

Weaving on a Fruit Lug

A shallow wooden box such as those used for packing grapes, pears, and other fruits may be made into a simple loom. The size of the woven material produced will depend upon the size of the box. The cloth may be used as a table runner, a place mat, or folded and lined to make a purse or envelope bag.

Two or three large smooth shuttles will be needed, each several inches longer than the width of the loom.

Rug yarn, or other heavy cotton yarn, weaves quickly and makes an attractive mat. Choose several colors, either harmonizing or contrasting, and plan stripes in the woven material, with various widths of alternating colors. Such color combinations as brown with beige, chartreuse and pumpkin yellow, and pearl gray with fuchia, pink, and purple make fabrics of unusually rich appearance.

To make the loom, smooth the top surfaces of the ends of the box with sandpaper. Down the center of each end, mark off one-half-inch spaces. Drive a one-inch wire brad on each mark, allowing them to extend one-half inch above the surface.

Tie the selected color of yarn to the first nail, take it down to the oppsite end, around two nails and back to the first end. Continue threading around two nails and back to the opposite end and around two nails. Cut the thread and tie it off on the last nail. This method of threading around two nails, across the loom and around two nails, etc., makes the warp threads lie alongside each other perfectly straight across the loom.

Wind a shuttle with another color and weave it over one thread, under one thread, over one thread, under one thread,

71

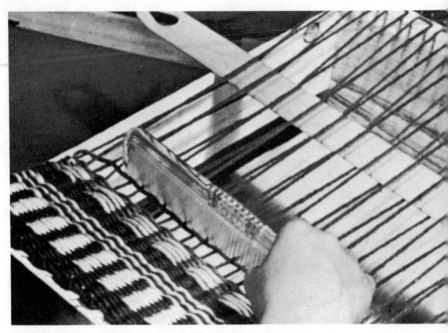

Fig. 44   Using a Heavy Comb to Pack the Weft

etc., across the warp threads. A ruler can be inserted in the
warp threads to facilitate weaving from left to right. Put the
ruler in, over, under, over, under, etc. Leave it in place as
shown in Fig. 44 and slide the shuttle through the shed made
by turning the ruler on edge. The threads may be easily picked
on the right to left throw of the shutttle.

The ends of the weft threads should be returned and hidden
in the weaving. When a new thread of the same color is joined,
the threads should be overlapped for a distance of about two
inches

Alternate colors in stripes of varied widths for a more
interesting design. Often an unusual effect is gained by using
threads of two colors at the same time, passing the shuttles
through the sheds alternately. This method of using two shuttles
results in a block effect. Fig. 44 shows black for several shots
across the loom, then black, white, black, white, etc., to produce
a block effect. Notice how the comb is used to pack the warp

loosely into place. The smooth shed-stick is allowed to remain in the warp to facilitate the weaving from left to right.

Another interesting effect results when one color is woven over two threads, under one, over two, under one, etc., for one row or shot. This type of skipping must be followed by two shots or passes across the loom in regular under and over weaving, or tabby.

Care must be taken when weaving on a fruit lug to be sure that the selvage edges are not drawn in. If the web does begin to draw in, take out the tight threads and re-weave, allowing the weft to turn loosely at the edge. If the edge persists in drawing in, drive long nails along the sides of the box and hook the edge threads of the warp over the nails to hold the edge of the web even with the edge of the box.

When the mat is woven, pull it up off the nails and trim off any surface ends of joined threads.

An interesting variation on this type of weaving might be to place the nails at quarter-inch intervals . . . remembering to pass the warp thread around two nails as before. This method of warping will result in a finer mesh fabric. The weaving is the same.

One might try some of the various knot techniques, such as tying in lengths of extra threads—or passing a shuttle across two threads, using a shuttle wrapped of several colors of threads, all wrapped together on the same shuttle. Instead of one color, such as blue, choose several shades or various intensities of blue . . . or wind together on one shuttle a dark red thread, an orange-red thread, a yellow-red thread, and a pink thread. When these various hues are wrapped together and woven together as one, the resulting fabric shows a more scintillating gleam of color . . . . and so is more interesting.

CHAPTER II

Weaving With Loopers

Looper weaving is a method of interlacing rayon or cotton jersey loops to weave a mat about seven inches square. The jersey loopers may be purchased at almost any store where knitting and crocheting threads are sold. They are manufactured by knitting mills in a wide range of colors.

Weaving jersey looper pot holders is an excellent recreational pastime for children eight or more years of age. When the child measures, cuts, saws, and finishes his loom himself, the weaving project is even more interesting.

Fig. 45   Driving the Nail in the Looper Loom

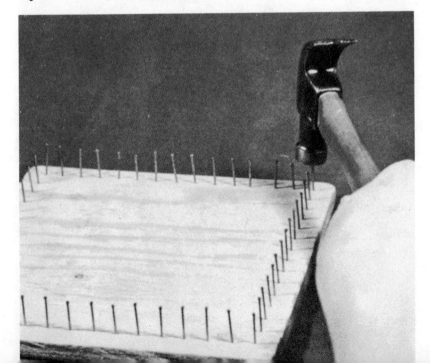

Many articles may be made from the woven mats; pot holders, small purses, and even place mats by joining several of the seven inch squares together.

To build the looper loom, secure a piece of one-half-inch plywood, eight inches square. Sand it smooth and draw lines one-half inch from all four sides. Mark one-half-inch divisions along each side and drive wire brads into the wood at these points, allowing them to extend about one-half inch above the surface of the board. There will be fifteen nails across each side of the loom, Fig. 45.

Mats may be woven in many patterns, but a plaid mat makes a very informal and colorful kitchen aid.

Select loopers of several harmonizing colors and test them across the loom to see that they are long enough to cross the loom from side to side.

Thread the loom by stretching loopers across in one direction, changing colors as desired. Notice the pattern for a plaid

Fig. 46   Weaving the First Looper

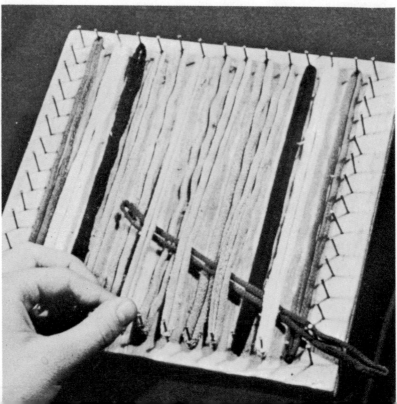

Fig. 47   Removing the Finished Mat

mat in Fig. 46. This shows the loopers stretched across the loom in one direction.

When the warp loopers are stretched across the loom, hold the loom so the warp threads are all vertical to the weaver. Select a looper of the same color as the edge color of the warp, and weave it through: over a looper, under a looper, over, under, etc., across the loom. Consider a looper as both sides of the jersey loop, Fig. 46. Catch the end over the first nail on the opposite side of the loom.

The second weft looper is woven on the other tabby, or under, over, across the loom and is looped over the second nail on each side of the loom.

Continue to weave across the loom until all the nails hold a looper. All of the weaving is plain weave, or tabby.

A large crochet hook, or a wire hook, is very helpful in removing the mat from the loom. Pick up a corner loop, slip it up off the nail, and catch the next loop through it. Hook the next loop up off the nail and catch it through the second loop, thus chaining the loops together around the edge of the mat, Fig. 47. If it is difficult to keep the unfinished edge on the nails while the mat is being removed, loop some of the already finished edge back on the nails for safe-keeping. When the chain edge is complete, except for the last loop in the corner, and the mat is loose from the nails, attach an extra looper in the last corner loop to use as a hanger.

Often a young child will be willing to try looper weaving, when all other types of weaving seem too difficult. This type weaving has been used successfully with children as young as five years.

Through the use of various colors of loopers, plaids and checks may be worked out to fit into any kitchen color scheme. In kitchen use, the cook will find these mats superior to anything ever used for a pot holder.

CHAPTER 12

The Twine Rug

The knot used to produce the pile or shag in this type of rug-making is the Giordes knot, used and loved by weavers through the centuries.

A very decorative and serviceable rug is made with twine or heavy jute as the foundation and knots or shag of heavy cotton roving about the diameter of a pencil.

The box which forms the loom is the type used for packing fruit. Remove all the nails around the top edges and sand this surface smooth. In the center of each end of the box drive a nail, allowing it to extend above the top of the box about one inch, Fig. 48. Tie the ends of the twine from two spools of heavy jute around the lower nail. Stretch these two ropes across the box and wrap them securely around the other nail. The two ropes will lie very close together across the top of the open box.

A piece of heavy cardboard measuring three inches by five inches is used as a guide in cutting the pieces for the pile or shag. Select cotton roving in three or four harmonizing colors. For a bedroom rug or bath mat, combinations of white, pink, rose, and gray would make an attractive rug. Cream, beige, and coral is another excellent combination.

Using the color which is to be in the center of the rug, wind the heavy yarn around the measuring card as in Fig. 49 and cut three-inch lengths with a pair of sharp shears. Any other method of measuring and cutting the three-inch lengths would be satisfactory.

79

Place a piece of the heavy roving across the two ropes. Draw the ends between the ropes and pull them up, towards the weaver. Slide this Giordes knot down to the front end of the box. Continue to tie knots, easing them along the ropes as in Fig. 51.

Fig. 48   Stretching Twine

Fig. 49   Cutting Shags

Fig. 50   Placing the Pile Over
the Binder Twine

Fig. 51   Tying the Giordes
Knot

As the rope stretched across the box becomes covered with knots, release more rope and move the two strands across the box. As the rug progresses, the ropes are moved again and again. The knot-filled strand winds around and around the entire rug.

When the finished length is about two yards long, it is ready to be bound together. For a small oval shape rug allow fifteen inches for the center color. Overcase the rope on the underneath side with heavy cotton carpet warp threaded through a large-eyed tapestry needle. Turn the corners rather loosely

Fig. 52   Lacing the Rug

so the edges of the rug will lie flat. If the rug begins to curl or cup, cut out the binding string and sew it again, allowing both the cords to lie flat. Arrange the placement of the colors from the right side, Fig. 52A.

The shag knots should not be packed too closely together on the ropes, or the rug will not lie flat on the floor.

The colors selected may be used at intervals throughout the rug, or they may be used in solid spots. For example, the center of a round rug might be a soft beige, surrounded with a band of light green, followed with medium green, with an edging of several rows of dark green.

This type of rug makes an interesting group project. One person can cut fringe, another can tie the knots on the ropes, and still another can lace the rug together.

Fig. 52A   Arranging the Rug Coil

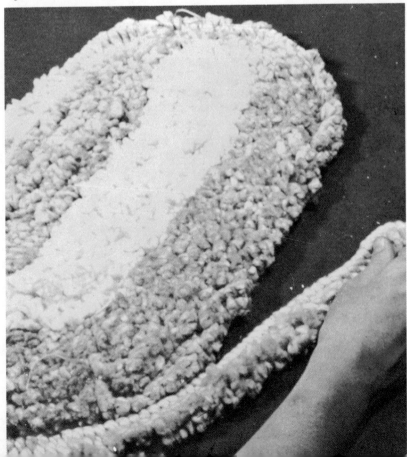

A Shag Rug Woven on an Orange Crate

An orange crate makes a simple loom for weaving mats measuring fifteen by thirty inches. Two or more mats may be overcast together to make a rug for the bathroom.

To prepare the orange crate, remove the nails and tin strips used to close the crate, and sand the top edge of the box smooth. Mark along the top edge of both ends of the crate at one-half-inch intervals. Drive one-inch wire brads at these points, allowing them to extend one-half-inch above the box.

Fig. 53 Warping the Orange Crate Loom

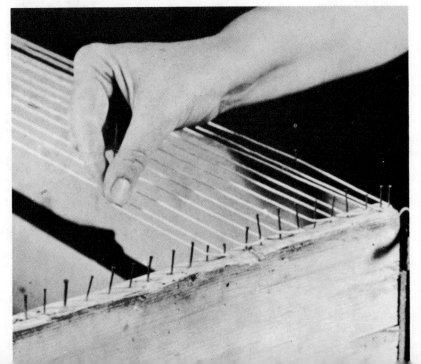

Attach small screw eyes at the four corners of the box, either
in a vertical position like the nails, or at the sides as shown
in Fig. 53. Heavy #8 metal clothesline wire is placed through
the screw-eyes and the ends turned at an angle. A metal rod
is better than the wire, if it is available. These metal rods help
to keep the selvages straight while weaving. Each weft of yarn
must pass around the rod.

Lightweight cotton yarn similar to rug yarn is used for the
warp threads and heavy cotton filler yarn for the weft threads.

Fig. 54   Tying the First Row of Shags

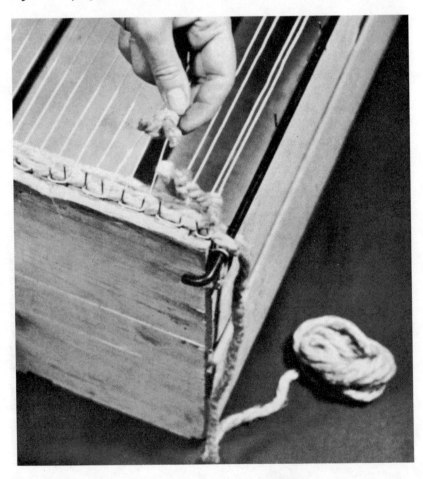

Borders of harmonizing colors add interest to the finished rug. the beauty of which depends upon color and texture.

The rug shown in Fig. 55 is being made with shags of deep green around the edge, a band of light green next to the deep green, and a yellow center.

Other color combinations might be beige with tan and brown, light blue with royal and deep blue, or cream, peach, and white. The choice of color depends largely upon the use of the rug. The soft fluffy surface of the rug makes it an excellent bath mat which readily absorbs water. If constructed from a good quality cotton filler, it will be wash-fast.

Warp the loom by tying the end of a ball of soft rug yarn to the first nail at one end, Fig. 53. Take the thread across the loom and around two nails on the other end of the box, back across the length of the loom and around two nails again, until

Fig. 55 Trimming Slightly Uneven Shag Ends

the warp threads are all stretched in parallel lines across the loom. Cut the warp thread and tie it to the last nail.

Select the background color for the rug, and cut a three-yard length of this heavy cotton rug filler. Finger weave it over and under across the loom. Return the end of the weft by turning a three-inch end of the thread back and hiding it in the weaving. Always consider the metal rod as another warp thread, including it in each row of under and over background weaving.

When three rows across the loom are complete, begin the shags for texture. Use heavy cotton rug filler and prepare several three-inch lengths of the desired color. The three by five card will be helpful in preparing these pieces. The shag rows are added after each three rows of background weaving. Select the three-inch shag. lay it over the first two warp threads and bring the two ends up toward the weaver. This is the individually tied Giordes knot which was used in making the twine rug. This knot stays in place through cleaning or washing.

Be sure to finger weave three rows of simple tabby weaving, under and over and around the metal bar, between each row of shags. The tabby background is necessary to hold the rug together.

If a two-panel rug with a border is desired, a squared paper design may be worked out using one square to indicate one knot or shag. If two identical panels are made, each with the border along one side, they can be joined at the center and the seam will not show because of the shags.

When the weaving is finished, remove it from the orange crate by slipping the warp threads up over the nails. Overcast two or more panels together. The use of squared paper in planning a more elaborate design lends itself to a very creative design and more original use of color.

The weaving on the finished rug may seem to be a bit open and loose, but when the rug has been in use a few days it packs and the threads unwind slightly to give a lovely texture.

CHAPTER 14

Ojibway Indian Bag Loom

This unusual loom is easy to build and use. The Ojibway Indians used this type of loom to make tightly woven bags of rushes and vines, probably for storing grain.

The loom consists of a flat base board upon which are mounted two upright dowels. These are braced across the top with a third piece of dowel or a small flat board.

The materials needed for weaving are harmonizing colors of heavy cotton rug filler and several yards of heavy smooth cord. Choose such combinations as black, red, and gray; dark green, tan, and yellow; or gray, rose, and blue.

Secure a piece of one-fourth-inch plywood twelve inches by four inches for the base of the loom. Cut twelve-inch lengths of one-half inch dowel rod for the uprights. These are placed eight inches apart, Fig. 56, and attached to the base with wood screws. Fasten a small bracing board across the top with short nails. In Fig. 56 a piece of dowel was used across the top with the corners smoothed down with wood filler.

The first step in making a shopping bag is to wind a strong, heavy cord around the top of the loom four or five times, and tie together, Fig. 56. Use thumb tacks to keep the strong Navy-type cord about one-half inch below the top of the loom.

Each warp thread of heavy cotton rug filler is twenty-five inches long. These are folded in the center, the loop placed over the cord and the two ends pulled through, Fig. 57. These snitch knots form an interesting rim or top edge on the bag. The colors may be placed in groups or their location may be planned to

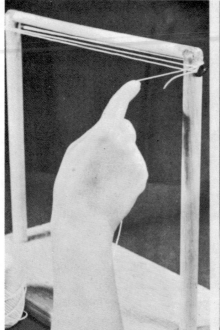

Fig. 56 The Ojibway Indian Bag Loom

Fig. 57 Warping the Ojibway Loom

Fig. 58 Twisting the Weft on the Ojibway Loom

match the colors on the opposite side of the bag. All the cord is filled with the warp knots. A string of several strands of heavy cord should be attached to each side of the bag for handles. Fig. 58. This cord handle may be covered with cotton filler before the weaving begins or after the bag is taken off the loom. The buttonhole stitch makes the handle comfortable and has good wearing qualities.

The weaving is done by crossing or twisting two weft threads around each pair of warp threads. Begin by placing a loop of weft thread around the first pair of warp threads, Fig. 58. Cross the ends of this weft thread and bring them around the second pair of warp threads. Cross them again and pass around the next pair of warp threads. Proceed to cross or twist the two weft threads all around the bag. Additional wefts are woven in this same manner. Open spaces may be left with the warp threads forming a lattice-like opening, Fig. 59. This is often done when a new color is begun.

Weave or twist down to within three inches of the ends of the warp threads. Knot the ends of the weft threads and cut off the extra length.

Fig. 59   Closing the Bottom of the Ojibway Bag

Fig. 60   Buttonhole Stitch on the Handle of the Ojibway Bag

Remove the thumb tacks and slide the bag up over the top bar. Finish the bottom of the bag by tying the warp threads together. Tie the threads on the front side of the bag with the corresponding threads on the other side of the bag, using a double knot, Fig. 60. After the warp threads are tied securely, into a fringe, the ends may be trimmed evenly with scissors.

If the handles of heavy cord were not previously covered with buttonhole stitch, this should now be done, Fig. 60.

These Ojibway bags make good book carriers and are also useful for carrying trinkets of all kinds.

CHAPTER 15

Inkle Weaving

The word *inkle* means narrow strip or band. Some authorities say the inkle loom was found among the effects of early colonial settlers around Salem, Massachusetts, The narrow band of geometric design may have been used for suspenders, garters, and other places where a strong, tightly-woven, tape-like band was needed.

The loom may be built at home or in the shop, but it must be very sturdy. Commercial makes are usually well constructed and inexpensive, Fig. 61. The weaving is fascinating. The two sheds are made by pushing down or up on the warp with the left hand.

The material used should be a smooth shiny thread, such as a #3 pearl cotton, because a loosely twisted thread becomes rough in the weaving. The threading of the loom is more difficult than the weaving.

The width of the finished strip or band depends upon the size of thread used and the number of threads used in the warp.

To plan the warping of the inkle, make two rows of squares with one more than half as many squares as there are to be threads in the warp. In the belt pictured in Fig. 62, 33 threads of #3 pearl cotton were used.

If three colors are planned for the warp, use the same color at each side of the loom. In other words, the placing of the colored warp threads should be symmetrical as in card weaving. The warp threads should be two yards and ten inches long, so that the finished belt will be long enough to fringe the ends and tie like a sash. The woven strip may be shorter if it is to be fastened to a buckle.

In threading the loom, alternate warp threads are passed through the small heddle loops. The weaving is done by pressing

Fig. 61   Threading the Inkle Loom

the hand on the entire warp, opening the sheds through which the shuttle passes.

Choose three colors for a simple belt of thirty-three threads, for example, brown, orange, and yellow. This combination of colors would enhance a natural color linen dress. Make a diagram of the color and threading plan using the two rows of

Fig. 62 Pushing Down Warp for First Shed

squares. The top row indicates the threads which do not run through the heddle loops. The lower row indicates the threads which are in the heddles. Use *B* for brown, *O* for orange and *Y* for yellow. The colors might be placed in the color plan something like this:

1	2	3	4	5	6	7	8	9	10	11	12	13	14	15	16	17
	B		O		Y		O		Y		B		Y		O	
B		O		Y		B		B		O		O		O		B

Number *17* indicates the center thread in the belt warp. The threading on the right side would be the reverse of that shown for the left side. Each length of warp must be individually cut and tied on the loom. Before threading, cut the required number of lengths of each color, each two yards, ten inches long. Attach one end of the first thread to the first dowel with scotch tape and thread the other end through the heddle loop, up over the top, around the back of the loom, down under the middle dowel, around the variable dowel, and tie the ends together at the front of the loom, Fig. 61.

The second thread is also brown. Tape one end in the same way just beside thread *1*, but do not follow the first thread up over the first top dowel. Place it straight across the loom from the beginning dowel to the back top dowel. These even threads (top row in the diagram) do not pass through the heddles. All the threads are the same length and, except for the heddle threading, follow the same path across and around the loom. Each warp thread is tied together, making a circle of the loom. The tape is used only to hold the end until the thread can be placed on the loom in the proper position.

Continue to thread the loom, following the diagram, until the *17* threads have been tied on. Then read back across the pattern from right to left, or 16, 15, 14, etc. The 17th thread is in the center of the belt. Do not place two of these threads on the warp.

When all *33* warp threads are in place, they should slip around the loom together. Wind a shuttle, either a flat stick shuttle or the inkle shuttle furnished with the commercial looms, Fig. 62. The weft thread may be the outside color of the belt warp. In this case, it would be brown. To weave, hold the left hand just back of the heddles, flat on the warp as in Fig. 62. The warp threads not held by the heddles will slip down and a

Fig. 63　Pushing Up Warp for Second Shed

shed will open through which the shuttle may pass. Then place
the left hand under the warp threads behind the heddles and
press the threads up. A new shed will open. Pass the shuttle
through. The inkle shuttle may be used to pack the weft threads
straight and tight across the loom. Continue to weave back and
forth across the band, drawing the selvage edges smooth and
straight. As the weaving grows closer to the heddles the wire
pins in the variable dowel may be removed, loosening the warp
so that it may be moved forward around the loom. Tighten the
warp, replace the pins, and proceed to weave.

Designs may be varied by picking up, with the shuttle,
certain colors of threads from the lower shed.

When the belt is finished, the warp threads may be cut at
the knots and the weaving removed from the loom. The ends
may be braided and trimmed, or a buckle may be attached and
a point stitched at the opposite end.

Inkle weaving is so much fun and goes so fast once the loom
is threaded that everyone should try it!

CHAPTER 16

Cardboard Weaving

There is a method of weaving a flat mat on a piece of corrugated cardboard, easily obtained from a large soap box or carton . . . . a packing case. The cardboard should be smooth and unmarred, and a suitable size place mat is 12″ x 18″.

Measure the cardboard and cut with a serrated knife along a penciled line. Measure and mark ½″ intervals around all four edges, one-half inch from the edge. Punch holes with a sharp darning needle or a thin nail. Tie a piece of cotton string at one corner, and bind the edges with a single binding in each hole, and a double binding at the corners.

Since these binding strings are to be cut off, to release the finished piece of fabric, many bindings may be used.

Begin to warp the cardboard loom by tying on to a corner binding a three-yard piece of heavy yarn. The illustrated fabric has a wool carpet yarn for warp and weft. Use a heavy yarn needle and bring the warp thread across the length of the cardboard and through an opposite string loop, then back through the first or tying-on loop. This puts a double thread from one end of the cardboard to the other. (See Fig. 63A) By threading back through the first loop before going on to the next string loop, the double warp threads will be horizontal rather than in a zig-zag arrangement.

Tie knots in the warp threads as more warp is needed to cover the entire surface of the board with double horizontal warps. The ends of the knots can be hidden in the web.

The weft threads are carried back and forth either with a

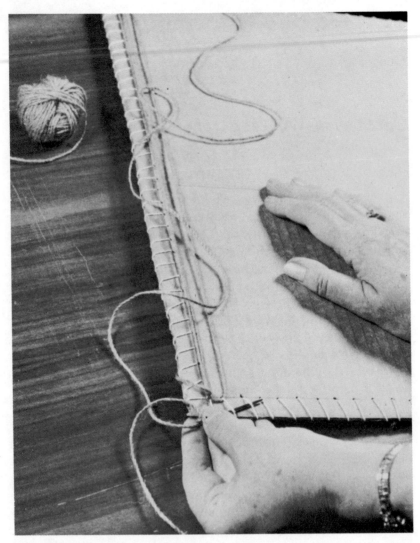

Fig. 63A Warping the Cardboard Loom

yarn needle or with a sharpened toothbrush handle. These little "needle-shuttles" can be very useful for a variety of weaving, and are made by breaking off the discarded brush, and sharpening the broken end on a file, and finishing with sandpaper to a smooth sharp point. As the weft threads move over and under, from side to side on the cardboard, it may be necessary to include the string holding loop several times, especially if the fabric is to be a solidly woven piece. See Fig. 63B. If scraps of harmonizing colors are used, it makes a balanced placemat to weave at both ends of the loom. So if there are ten rows across the loom of a yellow-green, then turn the loom around and weave

Fig. 63B   Weaving on the Cardboard Loom

Fig. 63C   Removing Fabric from the Cardboard Loom

ten rows across the loom of yellow-green at the other end. When the piece is finished, and a row of binding in a matching color has been added across the ends, the binding strings are all cut from the back side, and the finished piece of fabric is lifted off the cardboard. See Fig. 63C.

Various techniques may be used to give variety to the weave. It might be found interesting to use the cardboard loom for weaving a wall hanging with a see-through background—with various shapes woven in solid. If this is used, a steam pressing on the cardboard before the bindings are clipped, will help hold the threads in their position.

CHAPTER 17

Threading the Two Harness Loom

Very seldom will two weavers agree in their method of threading the simple loom. The method described here is fast, and several people may work on the loom at the same time.

The loom shown in the photographs is a twelve-inch loom equipped with string heddles and a size 15 reed, which means 15 threads per inch.

This threading method is of particular value when a chain warp is to be tied on at the front of the loom. Much time is saved if the heddle-threading and reed-sleying are already done.

Threading cords are tied in bunches on the warp beam at the back of the loom, and these cords are brought through the string heddles and across through the reed, one by one. Three people may work on the threading at the same time.

Cut two-yard lengths of natural color, cotton carpet warp in groups of ten threads. Fold these ten threads in the center, lay the loop over the back beam, and pull the ends through the loop, Fig. 64. This is a snitch knot. Continue to knot groups of threads on the back beam, spacing them across the dowel. Be sure the thread comes up *over* the frame of the loom so the threading cords lie across the loom in a straight line, Fig. 65.

One person may stand at the back of the loom to select a thread from the first group. Another may stand at the side of the loom to place the thread through the eye of the first string heddle on the *back* harness. He catches the thread around a threading hook held by a third person, who keeps the hook moving along the reed and fills each dent with a thread.

The second thread is selected from the group, passed through the eye of the first heddle on the *front* harness, and then hooked through the second dent in the reed. If the hook is held hook-up, the threads may be more readily pulled through. Fig. 65 shows the second thread being passed through the first heddle on the front harness. Notice that thread one has already been put through its heddle on the back harness and is already in the reed, where it will hang until the loom is completely threaded.

Continue to thread the loom, selecting any of the threads in the separate groups, bringing each thread straight across the loom, through the heddle, and then through the reed. If any threads are twisted around each other between the heddles and the reed, they must be corrected or the loom will not make a perfect shed for the shuttle to pass through when the weaving begins.

Fig. 64   Attaching Groups of Threading Cords

Fig. 65   Threading Eyes of Alternate Harnesses on the Two-Harness Loom

Notice that the string heddles slide along on the harness rods very easily. If there are more string heddles than required, they may stay on the loom. The wing nut in Fig. 65 tightens and loosens the action of the roller handle. When all the dents are filled with threading cords, there will be 180 ends hanging from the beater.

Any type of warp threads may be tied to these cords for weaving, Fig. 66. For example, suppose a scarf is to be woven. Tie onto each threading cord a two-yard length of fine green wool. The knots joining the threading cords and green wool warp are quickly slipped through the dents as the winding of the warp on the back beam begins. As the winding continues, the knots slide easily through the heddle eyes. The warp should be wound tightly on the back beam, with strips of paper separating each layer of the warp threads. All the threads should be placed smoothly and close to the center of the beam, away from the edges of the paper where they are likely to slip off and wind down around the ratchets.

After the green scarf has been woven, the knots of the threading cords are pulled through the heddle eyes and through the beater, then the scarf is cut off on the threading cords. This leaves the cords hanging in the front of the beater ready to have another warp tied on.

This method eliminates re-threading the loom each time a new warp is wound on the beam.

Fig. 66　Sleying the Reed with Threading Cords

Glossary of Weaving Terms

Beater — Frame to hold the reed. Used to "beat" weft threads into place in the web or woven cloth.

Chain — Group of warp threads as taken from the warping frame and chained to shorten and prevent tangling.

Cross, portee — Alternate crossing of threads at end of warp during winding to form a build-up, so threads may be selected one-by-one.

Dent — Single space in a reed.

Dressing — Preparing the loom, ready to weave.

Ends, warp — Cut ends of warp at the end of the chain.

Harness — Frames on which heddles are hung.

Heddles — Twine, wire, or flat pieces of steel with holes or eyes in center through which warp threads are placed.

Hook, warp — Flat metal hook used to pull warp ends through the reed.

Knot, snitch — Loop in thread through which both ends are passed.

Loom — Frame or machine of wood or other material on which a weaver works threads into a web.

Pick — Single shot of weft thread through shed across top of tightly stretched warp threads.

Reed — Comblike piece set in the beater to separate warp threads and used to beat threads together to form web. Usually made of fine metal.

Shed — Opening formed in warp, by raising or depressing treadles, through which the shuttle is passed.

Shot — Passage of shuttle through shed.

Tabby — Plain weave. Over, under, followed by under, over.

Taut — Tightly drawn threads.

Texture — Character or feel of finished web.

Warp — System of threads running lengthwise in loom across which weft threads are passed to form web or cloth.

Color Harmony Suggestions

The weaver should be especially alert for threads which will give a fabric a pleasant, or sometimes unusual, texture. There are glossy, shiny twists of all colors and gauges, yarns with dull flakes or bumps twisted into the length, loops or metallics added. The following color harmony suggestions will present endless variety when one considers the many types of yarns now offered for sale.

Since colors of full intensity are not usually considered harmonious some attempt at color description is made.

Triads
1. Bright yellow combined with pale blue and pale pink.
2. Bright blue, pale pink, yellow.
3. Bright green, pale orange, pale violet.
4. Bright violet, pale orange, pale green.
5. Yellow-orange, blue-green, red-violet.
6. Blue-violet, yellow-green, red-orange.

Analogous
1. Yellow, yellow-green, brown.
2. Orange, yellow, green.
3. Red-orange, yellow-green, blue-green.
4. Violet, red-violet, pale red-orange.
5. Blue, yellow-green, violet.

Monochromatic
1. Yellow, ivory, tan, brown.
2. Pale blue, royal blue, delft blue, navy.
3. Pale pink, rose, wine.
4. Pale green, green, dark green.

Single Color Harmonies
1. Red, white, black.
2. Light gray, dark gray, bright yellow.
3. Bright red, gray, black.
4. Bright pink, gray, black.

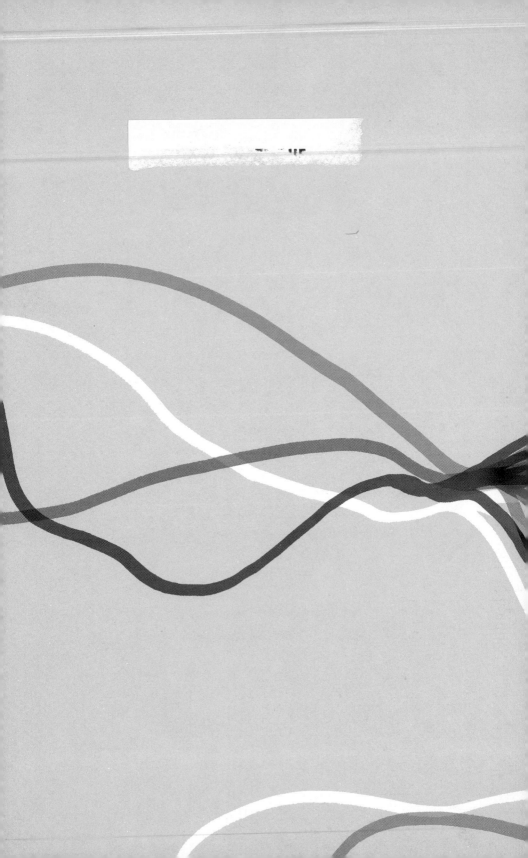